In the
of the
Comm

Out and About

The Post Office

Sue Barraclough
Photographs by Chris Fairclough

W
FRANKLIN WATTS
LONDON·SYDNEY

First published in 2006 by
Franklin Watts
338 Euston Road,
London NW1 3BH

Franklin Watts Australia
Hachette Children's Books
Level 17/207 Kent Street
Sydney NSW 2000

© 2006 Franklin Watts

ISBN-10: 0 7496 6914 4
ISBN-13: 978 0 7946 6914 0

All rights reserved. No part of this publication may be reproduced, stored in a retrieval system, or transmitted in any form or by any means, electronic, mechanical, photocopying, recording or otherwise, without the prior written permission of the copyright owner.

A CIP catalogue record for this book is available from the British Library.
Dewey Decimal Classification: 383'.42

Planning and production by Discovery Books Limited
Editors: Rachel Tisdale and Paul Humphrey
Designer: Jemima Lumley
Photography: Chris Fairclough

The author, packager and publisher would like to thank the manager and staff of the Victoria Square Post Office in Birmingham, and Alisha, Raz and Angela for their help and participation in this book.

Printed in Malaysia

Contents

The post office	4
The team	6
Starting the day	8
Managing the team	10
Waiting in the queue	12
Stamps and other business	14
At the counter	16
Forms and information	18
Sending a birthday card	20
Deliveries and collections	22
Sorting the post	24
Delivering the post	26
Closing time	28
Glossary	30
Further information	31
Index	32

The post office

People visit the post office to buy **stamps**, and to send letters and parcels. **Customers** come and go all day.

Post office signs are usually red, yellow and green.

People also go to the post office to pay in or take out money, pay their **bills** and buy things in the shop.

At the counter the staff help the customers to fill in forms and apply for **licences**.

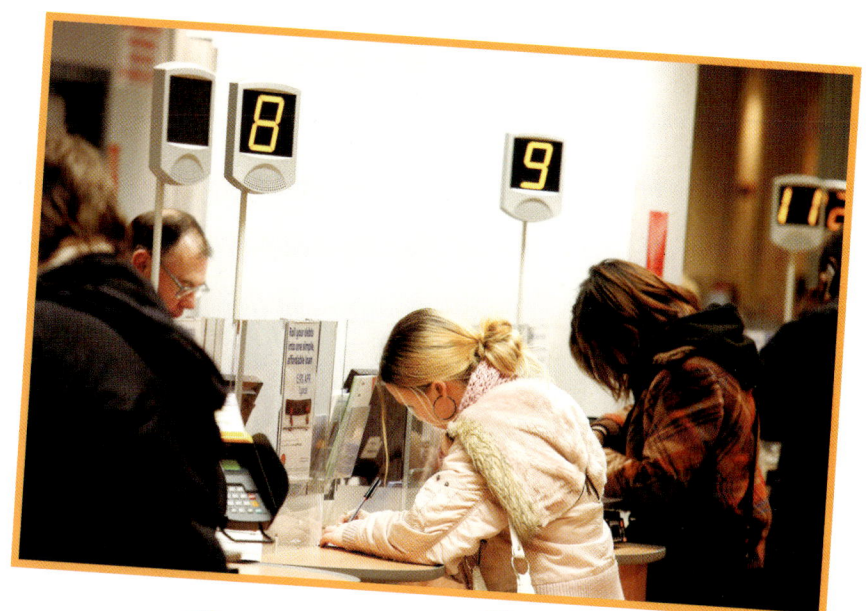

The team

A big team of staff is needed to keep the post office running smoothly.

The picture on the left shows Ian, the **manager**, and Thelma, the assistant manager. Managers make sure that there are enough staff working when the post office is busy. They also make sure that everyone has breaks during the day.

Most of the team work on the main counters. Some staff work in the **bureau de change**.

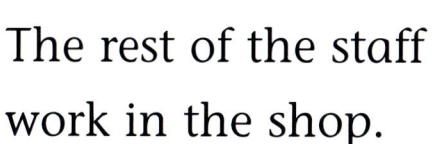

The rest of the staff work in the shop.

Postal workers

Postal workers come into the post office to collect all the post. They sort out and sign for the special deliveries. They make sure the post bags are loaded into vans and taken to the **mail centre** to be sorted.

Starting the day

Ian arrives early to open up the post office. All the other staff arrive to start their **shift**. There are plenty of jobs to do before the post office opens.

The shop staff make sure that all the shelves are tidy and full.

Ian often has a meeting with all the staff at the start of the day.

Once the post office is ready for the busy day ahead, the doors are opened. The first customers hurry in.

Soon the post office is full of people with post to send, or forms to fill in. A **queue** builds up as people wait for a counter to be free.

9

Managing the team

As manager, Ian has training sessions with his team. He tells them about new **products** and gives them all the information they need to pass on to customers.

At training sessions the staff use **role-play** to practise talking to customers, and test their knowledge of different products.

'Staff like team meetings as they get a chance to suggest new ideas.'
Brett, customer advisor

All the staff are trained to look after their customers. On the left, Thelma is helping Raz to tell a customer about a post office product.

Ian and Brett are having a chat about a change to the post office **website**.

Waiting in the queue

There are 17 counters at the main desk. The post office is often busy with a long queue of people waiting.

'Making sure we have enough staff for busy times is an important task.'
Ian, manager

The post office deals with huge amounts of post each day as well as **passports**, licences and **vehicle tax disks**.

Each counter has a number. When a **counter clerk** is ready for a customer, they press a button to announce that their counter is free.

Bags of post

Behind the counter, all the letters and parcels are stored in bags on trolleys. When the bags are full, they are tied up and put by the back door ready for collection.

Stamps and other business

Customers come in to buy stamps for their letters. There is also space for them to sit down and sort out their post inside the post office.

Thelma (left) tidies up scraps of paper that are left behind. She makes sure the post office stays clean and tidy.

'This is a busy office and customers need space to wrap and address items before sending them.'
Thelma, assistant manager

People also come to the post office to get money for trips to other countries. The bureau de change has most of the **currencies** that people need.

These are Swiss francs.

Special stamps

Sometimes the post office issues special stamps. They may have a certain theme or celebrate a special occasion. These stamps feature animal characters from children's books.

At the counter

Working at the counter is a busy job. Counter clerks use computers to help them track important letters and parcels, and to keep records.

Resham is taking a recorded delivery (see panel). The customer weighs the package to find out how much it will cost to send.

Resham puts the stickers and a postage label on to the package and takes the money. She prints a date stamp on the **docket** so the customer has a record of posting.

Special deliveries

If a package is urgent or important it can be sent by recorded or special delivery. This makes sure it is delivered faster or someone signs for it when it is delivered.

Forms and information

Every post office has shelves and racks full of forms and leaflets of information. They are carefully organized so that customers can easily find the form they need.

The post office is often full of customers filling in forms to apply for passports, licences and vehicle tax disks.

The racks and shelves often need to be filled up with new forms and leaflets.

Customers can come into the post office to ask for information. Naj (left) is trained to help.

Filling in forms

Most forms include a guide about how to complete them correctly, and have lots of boxes to fill with information.

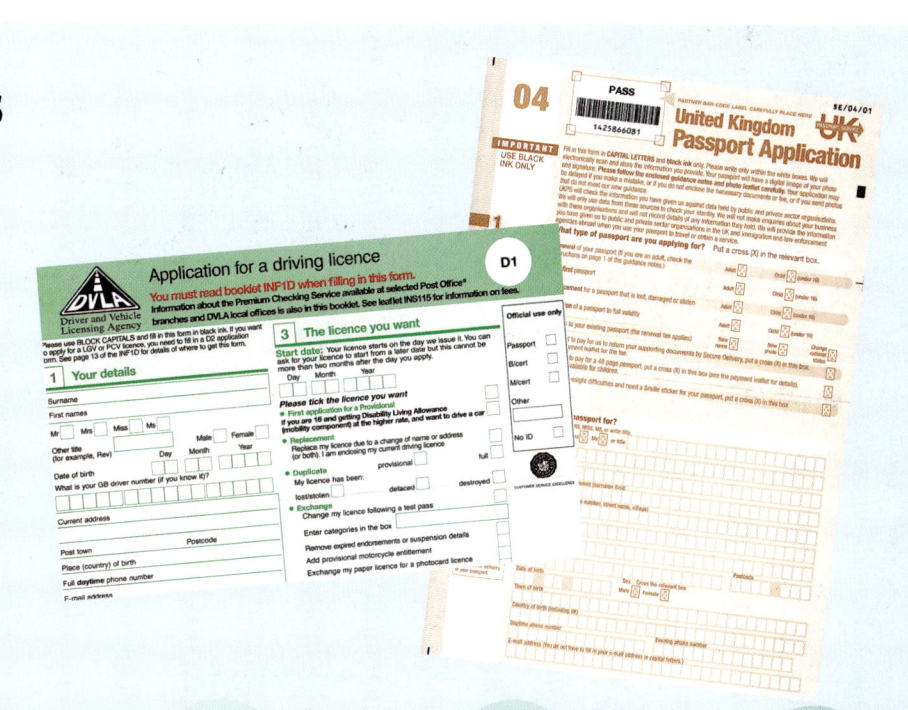

19

Sending a birthday card

Alisha is choosing a birthday card to send to a friend. There are lots of cards to choose from in the post office shop.

She takes the card to the till to pay and to buy a stamp.

Alisha writes a message in the card. Then she writes the name and address on the envelope, and sticks on the stamp.

Alisha posts the letter in the collection box in the post office. It drops down into a grey post bag.

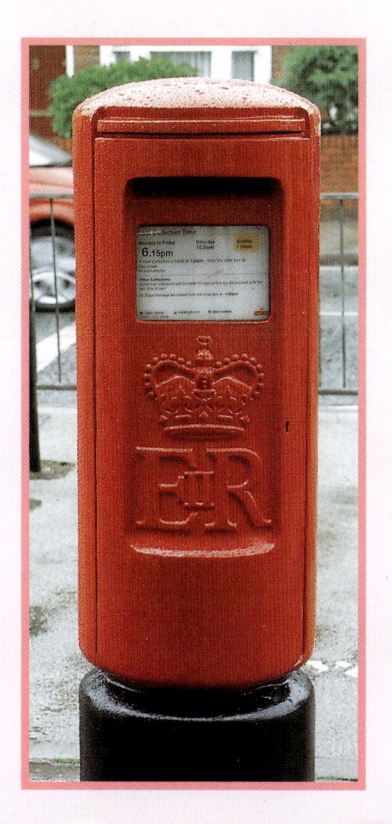

Post collection boxes

There is always a collection box at a post office. You can also post letters in a post box. These bright red boxes can be found all over the country, on busy city streets and quiet country roads.

The boxes are emptied by postal workers. The collection times are shown on the front of the box.

Deliveries and collections

Alisha's card and all the other collected post is put in grey post bags. When the bags are full they are tied up, ready for collection. The bags of post are collected by postal workers.

A postal worker also empties the box at the front of the post office.

All the post bags are loaded into a van and taken to a mail centre to be sorted.

Parcelforce

Parcelforce specialises in delivering parcels and boxes. This Parcelforce man delivers some boxes. Then he picks up parcels to take away in his van.

23

Sorting the post

The bags of post are taken to a mail centre. Huge piles of post arrive at the mail centre to be sorted day and night.

The bags are unloaded into trolleys and wheeled inside.

The post is put on to a **conveyor belt**. The letters go into a big drum that tumbles them and separates out bigger items to be sorted in a different place.

Alisha's card travels along to an automatic letter-facer. This machine turns all the letters the same way round, with the stamp at the top right-hand corner. Then it prints a **postmark** across the stamp.

'Careful addressing and using the postcode helps in speedy sorting and delivery of post.'
Ian, manager

The IMP machine

IMP stands for **Integrated Mail Processor**. This machine sorts the post by reading the **postcode**. Huge amounts of post can be sorted and processed very fast in this machine.

Delivering the post

Finally, the letters are sorted into areas according to their postcode. All the post for each area is sorted into its own box.

These letters are put into another bag and are transported by lorry, van or plane to a **delivery office** near their final destination. The bags of letters are unloaded at the delivery office.

Postal workers use a **frame** to sort the post for a delivery area. Mick (right) sorts Alisha's card with his other post.

Mick delivers his post on foot. He has put the post in his bag so that the letters to be delivered first are at the top.

Mick delivers Alisha's card. Her friend has been waiting for his birthday cards to arrive.

Closing time

In the afternoon, business customers arrive at the post office with post for the final collection.

The last few customers hurry in, just before closing time.

Raz closes down her counter so that she can sort out some important paperwork.

'At the end of a busy day we sort out our counters, ready for the next day's business.'
Raz, counter clerk

At closing time, Naj and Javed make sure that all the customers leave the post office.

Once the post office is empty, the staff pack up and get ready to leave. Thelma locks the front door and it's time to go home.

Glossary

bills documents that show amounts to be paid for goods and services.

bureau de change a special bank that buys and sells currencies for different countries.

conveyor belt a strip of fabric or rubber pulled along over rollers that is used to move things.

counter clerk someone who works behind a counter, sorting paperwork and helping customers.

currencies the notes and coins that people use to pay for things. Each country has its own currency.

customer someone who goes into a place to buy something.

delivery office a building where post is sorted before it is delivered.

docket a piece of paper that gives details of a parcel or package and shows proof of posting.

frame a set of pigeonholes that are used to sort post.

integrated mail processor a huge machine that is used to sort letters automatically by reading their postcodes.

licence a piece of paper that shows you have paid a fee to do something.

mail centre a building where post is sorted for different delivery areas.

manager someone who is in charge of running a place.

passport a small book that shows which country you are from. It is used to keep a record of travel, and has a photograph and other details.

postcode letters and numbers on an address that identify an area.

postmark a mark to show that a stamp has been used.

products things that are made and sold.

queue a line of people waiting their turn to do something.

role-play playing or acting a part to practise something.

shift a period of hours that people work.

stamp a sticker that shows an amount has been paid to post something.

vehicle tax disk a circle of paper that shows that a person has paid their vehicle tax. It is displayed in the front window of a vehicle.

website a series of linked pages of information on the Internet.

Further Information

Websites

www.royalmail.com Visit 'Stamps for Kids' to find out about stamps and collecting, and the latest stamp news.

www.postalheritage.org.uk The British Postal Museum and Archive. This is a useful site for news and information on exhibitions and events.

www.ukphilately.org.uk Philately is another name for stamp collecting. The 'Young Collectors' link has details of activities and workshops. See the 'Where to see stamps' page to find out about places to see stamp collections.

www.planetstamp.co.uk A good site for stamp news and quizzes, and some useful links to other related sites.

In Australia, visit: *www.aupost.com.au*

Every effort has been made by the Packagers and Publishers to ensure that these websites contain no inappropriate or offensive material. However, because of the nature of the Internet, it is impossible to guarantee that the contents of these sites will not be altered. We strongly advise that Internet access is supervised by a responsible adult.

Index

automatic letter-facer 25

banking 5, 7, 15
bills 5
bureau de change 7, 15

collection box 21
conveyor belt 24
counter 12, 13, 16, 29
counter clerk 13, 16
currencies 15
customer 4, 5, 8, 9, 10, 11, 13, 14, 16, 17, 18, 19, 28, 29

delivery office 26
docket 17

forms 5, 18, 19
frame 27

integrated mail processor 25

licence 5, 12, 18

mail centre 7, 23, 24
manager 6, 10, 12, 14, 25

Parcelforce 23
passport 12, 18
postage label 17
postal worker 7, 22, 27
postcode 25, 26
postmark 25
product 10, 11

queue 9, 12

recorded delivery 16, 17
role-play 10

shift 8
stamp 4, 15, 20, 25

team 6, 10

vehicle tax disk 12, 18

website 11